A Kaleidoscope of Verse

Dennis Lightfoot

With thanks to
Mary Gudzenovs for publishing assistance.

All images thanks to Pixabay artists.
https://pixabay.com

Dennis Lightfoot (c) 2023
ISBN: 978-0-6455080-3-1

INTRODUCTION

Much the same as each turn of a kaleidoscope the many diverse images and emotions – a narrative in verse – may strike differently according to one's outlook, personal situation or experience.

   The love of rural Australia and the search for a soul-mate have fed these diverse facets of verse. The author's path through life has been packed with a multitude of experiences; estranged family; country living; wild encounters and observations, all contributing to the kaleidoscope of poetry presented here. Some are humorous, some are descriptive and some delve into emotional depths to which a bruised individual might connect.

   Exposing one's soul can be a humbling experience but the author has entwined his life's highs and lows with a vivid, yet compassionate mindset. The reader may see revealed within the lines of these poems a glimpse of the multi-dimensional character of the writer.

TOWARD THE REASON
2015

Taking the soul through the pathway of life
To enrich understanding, tolerance, forgiveness
Form friendships, liaisons, involvement
Learn to love, respect, and nurture
Value freedom, honesty, and tranquility
Understand the meaning of happiness, achievement, family
Whilst avoiding the corrupt, the vexatious the hurtful

As the journey meanders through the unknown
Lessons from errors, poor judgment and oversights
Validate through obstacles, hurts, and heart aches
Lead to wisdom, self-worth and enlightenment
Bring about contentment, understanding and reality
Then genuine heartfelt love triumphs
Finally the soul has fulfilled its earthly destiny

To love and be loved – unconditionally

OVER THE HILL
1998

When you reach fifty
your hair still grows
not on your head
but out of your nose

Your waist keeps expanding
and your chest it goes flat
what once you called muscle
has now turned to fat

Your eye-sight is failing
and teeth are worn out
once they described you as tall
now they just say you're stout

Most of your joints are aching
your back has gone weak
you put your hand to your ear
to hear other people speak

You jog in the morning
to keep your self fit
but after five minutes running
you must stop for a sit

No more having a port
before going to bed
it's a hot cup of cocoa
your drinking instead

Now that your 'old'
and over the 'hill'
don't waste anymore time
upgrade your will

But when you have turned fifty
you can do magic at last
easily turn invisible
'cos young girls don't see you
when they walk past

DENIAL
2011

He stands at the counter
Waiting to be served
Beneath his calm public demeanor
A million thoughts and mental images
Subconsciously torment his mind
Gnawing on a multitude of past pains
Perceived injustice and a lost love
Fermenting as a darkness clouds his soul
Yet his composure hides that pain
Daily this pitiful existence is reinforced
With a smile and rehearsed replies
To store keepers and those he meets
"How are you today?" they may enquire
Once again his shallow ritual is repeated0
"I'm OK, thanks for asking"
Tactfully deceiving those around him
While his soul delves deeper into depression
That no-one would ever suspect

TAKE A LOOK INSIDE
1996

How are you really feeling
Is everything alright
Do you have good sleep
Or awaken through the night?

Has life given you plenty
Added much to your wealth
Granted all your wishes
Given you good health?

Is everything lovely
Happy , bright and fun
With nothing left unsaid
No deeds remain undone?

Do some aspects need changing
Are you set in your ways
With never a lonely feeling
Does love fill your days?

Can your heart sing its own song
One that's joyful, happy and keen,
Or is your spirit brooding
On what might have been?

To some, the questions are many
And the answers are few,
Words left unspoken
Perhaps now are due.

Love is the key
That opens up a heart,
The biggest step of any journey
Is the one at the very start!

THERE IS TWO OF ME
2010

External mask hides
Solitary me – within resides
Pontificate on what you see
Overlook the other me
Never shown or on display
Locked inside - tucked away
View only the facade that I show
The real me – who will ever know??

FROM SADDENED EYES
2000

From saddened eyes
a solitary tear
trickles down her cheek
like a dew drop
upon a pastel pink rose.

FRUSTRATION IS
2008

When does one know
To where they want to go
When can one see
Where they ought to be
When ones dreams are kept on hold
Seemingly never to unforld
When creative freedom is left behind
Overshadowed by the daily grind
Of chores, work and other things
That each day always brings
......This is — Frustration

PALETTE OF LOVE
2004

Splash me with gold
As summer days unfold
Beaches, sun, sailing

Tint me with brown
Autumn leaves carpet the ground
Holding hands, walking

Shade me in grey
Raining winter day
Cosy by the fire, snuggling

When it's spring
Brush me in a rainbow profusion
Bouquets of roses blooming
Painted from the palette of love

PERSEVERANCE
2022

Striving to convey to paper,
Those images
Held within the mind
Of memories,
Experiences and fantasy.

Exposing the soul,
To write the emotions of love
Captured within
Its tenderness, excitement and heartache.

The anguish of a frozen pen
Upon a blank paper
Then elation when
A sensual verse is born.
Such is the path of a poet.

SOCIAL OUTCAST
2009

Threads of shirt-sleeve cuffs
grimy tattered collars
layers of mismatched clothes
bulge from grubby ragged overcoat
discarded by those,
reminiscent of once he was.

Unkempt, unshaven, disillusioned,
he sits, introvert, staring,
alone, upon a park bench
avoiding disapproving eyes
of the well-to-dos,
resembling how once he was.

Cheap flagon wine
hunger and biting cold
painful memories
anesthetized with every lingering sip,
a social outcast,
rejected, but once he was.

Daylight fades into darkness,
icy airs chill
streetlamps cast eerie shadows
solitude in his park domain.
intoxicated, oblivious,
reliving dreams of when once he was.

THE JOURNEY
1992

Along the path of life we wander
Looking here and there,
Searching for that someone,
Someone who will really care.

Someone who will love you,
No matter what you do,
Someone who will be there
To help you see life through.

Someone with a quiet strength
With a heart of pure gold,
Someone who can see your needs,
Never having to be told.

Someone who does understand
Errors are a part of learning,
Someone to gently guide your steps
To help stop those faults returning.

Someone who shall only see,
Good in what you have done.
Someone who really knows
How the race of life is won.

Someone who is more than a lover
More than just a friend,
Someone who will be with you
...until the very end.

FROM START TO THE END
2022

First words, ma-ma and da-da
These evolve into names of
Family, relatives and friends
School and work mates
Some names stay
Some get forgotten
As time passes
Names of doctors, nurses and carer's
Become important
Until all that remains
Is a name carved into marble.

THE SALES REP
2008

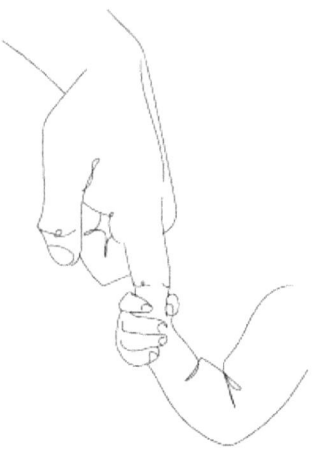

Motel room number 21
He sits tired, lonely
so ends another day
for the traveler
Up since dawn
On the road
Brief stops
At dots on the map
pushing to make a sale
To please the boss
Earning to support the family
By day he's a company man
Suit and tie
each evening he's Dad
just a phone call from home
tonight the phone keeps on ringing
no-one answers
where what and why
races through the mind
give it one more try
and dial again
ring, ring – ring, ring – ring, ring
hello, she says
is that you Daddy?

ANNIVERSARY
2009

Year after year
Has dissolved into time
She's gotten older
Hair turning grey
Never a week has passed
When she has not pondered
Why it had to be this way
The past has its pain
Etched into her soul
But what was done
Is hard to undo
There's an ache in her heart
That won't go away
And through the confusion of
Human reactions
An emotional chasm
Has come between them
Growing ever wider
Yet, she wonders if he still loves her
Will she ever know
Possibly never will
Anxiously she waits
On their anniversary
Perhaps this time
A note or a card
But once again tears flow
And lamentably
Another year passes

M - THE WIDOW
2002

As the beauty of her youth fades
lines of time now veil her
once silk smooth complexion
Grey invades the gloss of auburn hair
Suppleness has ebbed from yesterdays
curvaceous body
that presents itself today not as tall
when she was a younger woman

Maturity and the giving of life
to another generation
now reveals its cost
with creeping subtle vicissitudes
that dissolve time
pilfer years and partners
creates undeserved loneliness
in an empty house

Yet, looking into the windows of her soul
one sees smoldering embers
that still yearn
to love and be loved,
I ponder,
Who will now cherish this precious lady
hold her hand through the crystal years
and share her cappuccino.

ANOTHER YEAR PASSES - SHE
2009

Year after year
dissolved into time
she's gotten older
hair twilight streaked
never a week has passed
when she has not wondered
why it had to be this way?

The past has its pain
etched into her soul
but what is done
so hard to undo
an ache in her heart
that won't go away
does it have to be this way?

A confusion of reactions
the emotional chasm
between them
grows ever wider
and she wonders
if he still loves her
will it always be this way?

Anxiously she waits
on their special day
perhaps this time
a card or a note?
once again tears flow
her candle of life burns down
must it continue this way?

ANOTHER YEAR PASSES – HE
2009

Another year
Has slipped silently by
He's has aged somewhat
Hair turning to silver
Lines of time now show
Yet never a week has gone by
That he hasn't given thought
Why it could not change

The past is regretted
And the wounds remain
Now locked in a mundane existence
He's become resolved to living
Alone without a partner
While the ache in his heart lingers
And a sadness in his soul
That has never left

Through the confusion
Of human emotions
He wonders if her love still remains
But an ever widening chasm
Has come between them
No contact forthcoming
How will he ever know
If she might still have love for him

Possibly never will
And once again
Another year passes
With question unanswered
He lives in hope
With an aging heavy heart
Carrying a constant burden
And still wondering

SOLACE PENDING?
2009

Bygone days they were
Together
Years have gone perhaps
Forever
Once lovers close
Entwined
Wounded memories nowadays
Remind
Cherish care honour
Forgive
Permit the spirit freely
Live
Without chains of past that
Bind
Of love aggrieved
Remind
Heart felt pain hidden
Deep
True feelings interminably
Keep.
Yearning to be freed

AT DEATH
2019

When the flickering candle
Of this earthly life
Burns no more
Then begins our spirit journey
Into the unknown
Depths of infinity
Where a billion souls
Await the new beginning
Of their resurrection

AU REVOIR
2011

Keeper of souls
Take care of our loved one
Grant them a place
To rest in their peace
Bless them with eternal happiness
Wherever they have chosen
To be forever

Sentinel of spirits
Show them the same love
That flowed from their heart
Each day of their life
Guard them with care
So deserved are they
To be loved forever

Guardian of hearts
Nurture this sharer
This beautiful soul
Whose pathway of life
Now takes them to you
Until we can continue
Our journey together

WHY?
2023

Ponder the reason why
We were born to one day die
To fill those years in between
With experiences and much to be seen
Along the way involve others in our life
Parents teachers, friends, husband or wife
Run the gauntlet between sickness and health
Strive for happiness and hopefully gather wealth
Live with grey clouds that loom above
Or bask in the sunshine of a perfect love.
One has to wonder why???

DAD, WE LOVE YOU AND ALWAYS WILL...
2013

Where was this insidious disease hiding?
That stole his reasoning without warning
What happened to the cheerful dad?
We thought we knew so well
What is this vacant look?
In his loving blue eyes
How did this happen to the Dad
We adore so much
Please, oh please
Help us comprehend
His cerebral journey
Into the dark chasm of yonder
Where reactions fade
And recognition is lost

WHEN IT IS ALL SAID AND DONE
2020

Who will be there for you?
As your years fade into memories
Who will weep for you?
When your eyes close for one last time
Whose heart will be heavy with pain?
As they say goodbye forever
Who will that person be????

FRIENDS
2010

Good friends support
One and other
Goods friends lift
Each other when they are down
Good friends care
And nourish each other
Good friends endure
Through times of woe
Good friends freely
Give their love
Because
Good friends understand.
To have a good friend
Is to be one.

BIRTHDAY
2013

Another empty year
Slips into the void of time
Her once beauty fading
An unfilled life continues
Without him

Past pains
Scar her soul
With aching heart
She reminisces
Grieves his leaving

Today, her birthday
Her special day
Anxiously she waits
Perhaps this time
A card, a note, a rose

A splash of tears blur
Her one precious photograph
Despair fills her soul
Her candle of life, again

Burns slowly down without him

TWO WORLDS
2008

Three a.m.
Swathed in sepia darkness
She lay
Warm soft, oblivious
To his restlessness
His mind, processing problems
Musing perceptions
Pondering reality
Before quietly slipping
From their snug cocoon
Leaving her
To dream alone
He retreats downstairs
With bleary eyes
Enters
The electronic world
His parallel universe
Of Facebook
Google
Messenger
Twitter
To escape
At least
Until dawn
Then with bloodshot eyes
Meets another day
With nothing resolved

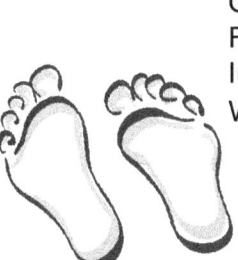

Our
Footsteps of existence
Imprint upon the soul
With each encountered experience

MUSING OF GROWING OLD
2010

It was just a couple of years ago
or that's what it seemed
I turned forty or so
A bit later fifty five was the number
on the card I received
Sixty came and went
so did my hair
But I didn't really care
So glad that I had got this far
Many of my mates had already passed
through the pearly gates
Life was shorter for those
Sad to see them go
Perhaps they were lucky
No more work or worry
Facing the bills
getting ill taking pills
for an age related ailment
of aches and pains
joints that don't work the same
Looks like I will have to go full term
Must have more lessons of life to learn
Maybe then I might retire
put the feet up
sit in front of the fire
glass of wine – a good book
reading or wasting time
waiting for the eyes to close
nothing more to do or see
At peace with my destiny.

SUMMER DAY DREAMING
2012

On the brightly coloured beach towel she sat
In the shade of a large straw hat
Zinc cream smeared neatly on her nose
Wriggling her painted nail toes
In soft warm sand at noon
While reading her Mills and Boone
Dreaming of a love she yearned

Nearby stood a handsome young man
Covered in oil and a bronze suntan
Observing the world from behind his sunglasses
Everyone and everything that passes
Women children and joggers with dogs
Speed-boats, jet-skis, swimmers in togs
All enjoying the sun

Looking up from the page she was reading
Her eyes not believing
The sight of this handsome Adonis creature
Possessing every feature
That she did ever desire
Her heart was now on fire
Next to her stood the man of her dreams

Perhaps if while out swimming
Could fake that she was drowning
He would bravely come and save her
Then she could return the favour
By offering him to dine and wine
With her feminine guile catch him on her line
Fall in love and live happily ever after

It wasn't long before her dream was shattered
And destroyed every thought that mattered
Someone was calling from further down the shore
Her heart was broken even more
When her Adonis walked away, hand in hand
With another equally good looking man
On that sunny afternoon...

AFTER SCHOOL
1999

Hungry tummy,
Explore the kitchen cupboards
Cake tin and 'fridge.
Crumbs on the table
Empty glass on sink,
Hurry outside

Backyard... adventure land,
Chase the dog,
Throw the ball,
On the swing
High as you can go

Loud voice!
Who ate the cake?
Come inside!
Clean your mess!
Change your clothes!
Shift your schoolbag!
Do your homework!

Cubby house
Good hiding place,
Sit on floor
Don't look out,
Mum can't see me.
Shoo dog, go away!

ÉCLAIR DREAMS
2020

Behind the glass counter it sat
He asked – how much is that?
For a moment he imagined biting
Into cream and chocolate - so enticing
His finger pointed to it from outside
Three dollars fifty - she replied
His heart suddenly sunk with horror
There was only a single dollar
In the pocket of his jeans
Thus shattering his seductive
Sweet éclair dreams.

YOU BRING THE BAIT...
AND I'LL PROVIDE THE BERLEY
1999

I was going for a harbour cruise, the other day
before we had left the wharf, I felt the boat begin to sway
To my seat I went and sat, very quickly
The movement of the boat , made me feel quite sickly.

I almost brought up my breakfast, I'd eaten an hour ago, at the most
now in my mouth I had the taste of coffee, juice and toast,
so I swallowed it back down again, while the captain of the boat
recited safety procedures, how to put on life vests
and how in an emergency, they would keep us afloat.

The sea looked cold and uninviting
one thing was for sure, I didn't want to take a boat trip
where I had to swim back to the shore.
The boat started up, then headed out to sea,
lots of yucky feelings, were going on inside me.

Each time I looked at the waves, my tummy started churning,
I was doing my very best, to stop my breakfast returning.
But then the boat, rocked and swayed and bucked,
over the side, my last meal,
with out further hesitation, I chucked.

This caused a reaction amongst the others,
 that on this boat ride came,
and twenty pale green passengers
were doing exactly the same.

The captain who was a canny lad
bought the craft to a sudden stop,
"grab a line and start fishing"
he said, as he anchored on the spot
Then announced to everyone , "the good news is,
today we should be home early,
and we will catch lots of fish,
because we did such a good job
of putting out the berley".

THE YACHT CLUB KING
2005

Dressed in blue Bermuda shorts
Soft soled Deck shoes
Calf length white socks
Topped off with a Captains' peeked cap.
He looks the picture of a seasoned yachtsman

Out into the bay he sails
Crew at the ready for the challenge
Man against the elements

Bracing himself against the thwart
With a vice-like grip on the helm
Sails close hauled
Strain at the clew
The keel slices emerald brine as the
Bow drives through the heaving swell
Toe-rail dips as she heels
Wash, streams aft along the deck

His face wet from spray
Salty tang stings lips and tongue
Weather eyes, watching, anxious
Waiting for the exact moment
To shout the command
"Ready to go about"

Adrenaline rises
Waiting, waiting, waiting
In anticipation of that
Vital last tack,
Then around the buoy
To run ahead of the wind
Spinnaker full to bursting

Cheers erupt from the crew
As he powers his yacht home
After braving all that nature threw at him
Claiming a heroes victory
In another Saturday arvo
Division 'A' yacht club race.

THE PAIN OF CHOICE
1999

When ever I go down to the pub
To have myself a drink
I always have to pause a while
And have a little think

What will I choose to quench my thirst
How big a glass should it be
Will I have just the one
Or maybe two or three?

Shall I have a beer or stout
Or imbibe a glass of wine
Perhaps I'll have a spirit
Or sip a liqueur oh so fine!

This happens to me every time
I'm sure it must hurt to think
Because next morning, I will surely pay
For having to choose what to drink!

My head will be truly sore
And my tummy feeling crook,
I reckon it's caused by that thinking
And all the time it took

Maybe, I should buy a keg of beer
And keep it at my home
Then I'll not have to think again
Until all of it has gone...

But, should I drink it from a glass
Or maybe from a jug
Oh heck! I've started to think again
Perhaps it's time I went
Back down to the pub!

THE OLD FARM UTE
1994

She wasn't brand new
when I first got it
and for many years
she went like a rocket,
my old farm ute.

There's a crack in the windscreen
the body's a bit rough
the tyres are bald
but she was built real tough,
my old farm ute.

It's taken me everywhere
across this land
through the rain, the mud
the dust and the sand,
my old farm ute.

I've driven her in the city
and in the great outback
just doing the shopping
or blazing a track,
with my old farm ute.

Now, she sits out behind
the back of the shed
with tyres all flat
and the battery gone dead
she was my old farm ute,

To me she will always be
that bloody beaut,
once trusty old,
now rusty old farm ute.

NO SEX
2015

He's got a ride on mower
A wide screen telly
He's overweight
With a beer-barrel belly
Keeps complaining
The diets aren't working
Knows its exercise he's shirking
Has to put down the stubby
Get off his arse
Take out the old Victa
Push-mow the grass
Or sign up with Jenny Craig
And start paying
Then he won't be saying
It's been ages since he's been 'laid'.

A FREUDIAN SLIP
1995

In to the supermarket
to do some shopping,
past the frozen goods
she went without stopping,
along the aisle to the deli section
looked in the sliced meat display,
to make her selection.
"Next please", came from the assistants lips.
"That's me, may I have some Frincon Litz,
Did I just say "Frincon Litz"?
Oh! I'm sorry, I wasn't thinking,
I would like some fritz
that's made in Port Lincoln".

This really happened to the lady to whom I was once married.

Lincoln Fritz was a product of the local
Port Lincoln Bacon Factory run by the Castley family
who traded under the name of Lincoln Bacon Specialists.

NIGEL NO-FRIENDS PARTY
2008

        For him another year has just passed
"It may as well be my last"
        He lamented and moaned
"Once again I'm stuck at home"
        By himself and all alone
"With no-one to share my special day"
        But who would care anyway
"I shall light the candles and cut the cake"
        The one he took all day to make
"Then I'll open a bottle of bubbly wine"
        To have himself a jolly good time
"I will blow a whistle and wear a party hat"
        And when he'd had enough of that
"Refill my glass and drink some more"
        Probably fall down on the floor
"Might as well" - he growled and hissed
        Opened the bottle and got pissed
"It's my party and I'll have all the fun"
        He doesn't need you or anyone
"Habby birthday to me"
        A sad and lonely sight
"Habby birfday to me"
        With an empty heart
        He kept on drinking all night long
        And singing his solo song
"Habby ---birfday----toooooo---meeeeeee

KEEPING IT HANDY
1999

When you go to Rossy's farm
You'll see the junk he's got
scattered around the homestead block,
there's really quite a lot.
At a glance one could tell
That junk must breed quite well
'cos you can see for sure,
the stuff is not getting less
in fact - it's getting more.

There's
Four old tractors with tyres gone flat
Seven wrecked cars dumped next to that
A motor bike that has no chain
Three farm Utes that won't go again
A couple of ancient horse drawn drays
That have seen much better days
Five combines that are seized
An ancient harvester full of bees
Two hay mowers that won't go now
And a broken stump-jump plough.

There's
Boxes of parts covered in dust
Everything metal is full of rust
Worn out tyres to fit cars and trucks
A wire crate for carting ducks
Twenty bags of super, that's gone hard
Bottles and tins scattered around the yard
Sheets of galvo full of holes
Rusty wire wound up in rolls
A lighting plant motor that doesn't run
And an empty 44 gallon drum.

To Rossy it's all his treasure
Just looking at it gives him pleasure
If you suggest to throw some away
In quick reply he'll say,
"Why do that - I might use it one day".

BLOOMERS
2010

Six white bloomers
Snow white bloomers
Fluttering the breeze
On grandmas washing line
Six white bloomers
Bleached white bloomers
In the bright sunshine

Grandma prides herself
For her whiter than whites
Puts them in the tub
Soaks them overnight
After a rinse and a scrub
She hangs them out to dry
They flutter proudly in the sky

Six white bloomers
Snow white bloomers
A pair for every day
Six days of the week
All but one
That's the pair
She still has on

Six white bloomers
Snow white bloomers
In the backyard sun

BLOODY FLIES
2000

Buzzing around your face
Crawling in your eyes
Riding on your back
A thousand bloody flies.

Landing in your food
Sitting on your plate
It's no wonder we hate,
Those bloody flies.

There's Blowies and Bushies
Blue-tails and House ones too,
Waiting out there, somewhere,
Just to bloody annoy you.

Brush them, swat them
They don't seem to care
Those persistent bloody flies,
Are every-bloody-where.

Spray them, zap them
They never go away
Those pesky bloody flies, I reckon,
Are here to bloody stay.

C'EST LA VIE
2001

Where to now? he ponders,
allowing life's ever changing path
to have its own freedom
being unattached
to whatever the outcome.
Thoughts of a 'maybe-love'
secreted away within,
awaiting events that may unfold,
without fear of gain or loss.
Perhaps this 'Goddess' demands
only total perfection, nothing less,
willing to sacrifice her yearning emotions
without ever tasting
one moment of intimate pleasure
from which to seek perspective
or to simply enjoy the experience
of a brief distraction
in the search for love.

MEMORIES
2010

As I watch the morning sunrise
I think of you
Listen to birds sing at dawn
I think of you
Inhale the scent of dew covered roses
I think of you

I still reminisce when
Your warm body
Graced my bed
Your sweet perfume
Lingered on my pillow
Where our bodies entwined
In a night of tender intimacy

I will always
Think of you

BEING INVISIBLE
1998

Ever been in a crowded party
feeling unseen by all,
wondering why everyone else is talking
no-one is bothering to talk with you?

They seem to be having fun
chatting, laughing and dancing,
while you just stand there, alone,
clutching in your hand, a glass of drink
with ice blocks beginning to melt.

You stand there, hoping that someone
will come over and start a conversation.
Your eyes scan the crowd,
going from one person to another,
eager to get some form of eye contact
so that you can at least feel accepted.

No-one even notices your existence,
they just keep on chatting with each other
while you stand there
still clutching that glass of drink,
with melting ice blocks.

Negative thoughts flow.
You question your choice of clothing,
"I should have bought that other coloured shirt,
is it my jacket, it can't be that far out of date, or is it?
perhaps it's my new cologne?
the sales person said "it was sure to attract the girls".

Hopefully you search the crowd for a friendly face
no-one passes a glance your way.
You envy those good looking 'in' people
with two or three eager listeners gathered around
laughing at every joke
you wonder what makes them so popular.

Maybe next time you see a magazine ad,
'the one that guarantees to make you more attractive',
you'll cut out and send the coupon.
Meanwhile you stand there,
pathetically clutching that drink,
ice blocks now melted... and feeling invisible!!!

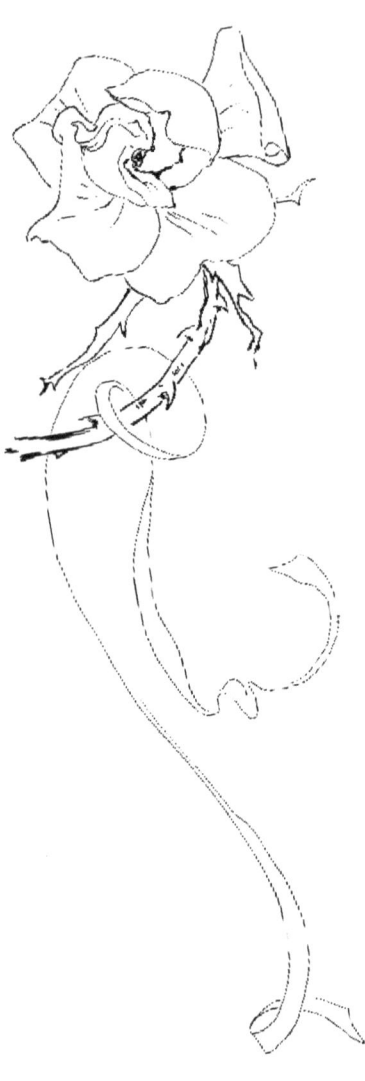

LOVERS
2013

He emailed her to plan a date
night out on the town it did indicate
come to her house she invited
he showered and shaved, all excited
she met him at her door
gave him a lingering kiss
that promised more
ate a dinner of pasta and wine
held hands most of the time
talked about friends and places to go
sat on the lounge
watched a video
she drank more wine
he drank more beer
seductively she said
"come over to here"
together they snuggled
in each others arms
he was infatuated
lost to her charms
lips together entwined
everything seemed just fine
then - ring ring on the doorbell
She cried , Oh heck oh hell
Its him – you have to go
My husband is home early - from Tokyo

THE BACHELOR
2014

He was a private man
That liked to be alone,
Spent most of his time at work
Or watching telly at his home
'Time had come' – he said to himself
I'd like to share my life with someone else
So out he went to find a mate
But she would have to be one
That he would highly rate
She must be a generous sexual partner
On this he would not capitulate
A young maid he did finally find
That met the criteria and mental image
He had in mind
She was beautiful
She was sweet
But he found she could not compete
With his other long time other lover
A blow up one
Made of silicone rubber

EMOTION
2000

Alone he stands
his gaze fixed upon
her name,
carved into marble.
A silent tear drop falls,
splashing upon
the polished surface.
His trembling hand
holds forth
twelve red roses...
"happy anniversary,
my love ".

IN ANOTHER TIME, IN ANOTHER PLACE
2016

Three decades seemingly vaporised into time
She went her way
He went his
The wheels of their emotions
Both travelled diverse roads
New experiences, altered destinies
Different lives, partners and families...
Yet, deep in his heart,
Among the cold ashes of the past
A faint ember flickered
At the mention of her name
Or the occasional a passing glimps...
Sporadically, without warning
Through his sleep, a dream may float
Where, for a brief moment,
They are together again
Then like a dawn mist,
That fragment of time evaporates,
Leaving him to wonder,
Does she ever experience the same?
alas mon ami

ETERNAL LOVE
1999

True love is of the spirit
Not an earthly thing
Something that cannot be bought
For the price of a shiny ring
True love cannot be broken
By some fault or misdeed
True love is eternal
If only you believe

Many that have loved and lost,
Gone their separate ways
Often burdened with aching hearts
That reminisce of love filled days
Yearning to understand
How to be pure of soul and heart
Wonder if ever they might
Return back to the start

True love is eternal
Fulfilling their spirits path
With something death cannot part
Or destroy the magic they possess
The gift that resides within in the heart
Soul-mates take a vow never to be apart
With this blessing from above
When one has found their perfect
Last forever love

FATE
2010

In our journey through life
We encounter others
Is it chance or destiny?

Some we meet
Excite our senses
Others we ignore

A precious few
Live in our hearts
Never to be forgotten

Our paths met
You touched my spirit
Gifted me with your love

In my treasures of life
Among the beautiful experiences
There will always be you

Thank you for caring and sharing
Enriching my life
Bought together by fate

FICKLE EMOTIONS
2007

Does the heart
Really know
In what direction
It should go
Is love
Simply a thought
That must be learnt
And can't be taught
Do those we meet
Along the way
Change our thoughts
In such a way
That emotions change
Day by day
So much that
In the end
What had began
As a lover
Is now just a friend

PASSION RISING
2001

They hug,
two become one
holding each other close.
Her sweet essence and soft, soft skin
fills his senses and
sends his heart pounding.
Slowly and tenderly he kisses
her neck, her cheek, her lips.
Her eager lips echoing his passion
he becomes totally lost to her
in this shared embrace,
and wishes, this kiss,
could last forever..

HAVE I TOLD YOU
1999

I could say
I love your eyes
Or the colour of your hair.

I could say
I love your smile
Or the clothes that you wear.

I could say
I love the shape
Of your body soft to touch.

I could say
I love the way you think,
But it wouldn't mean as much

As what I want to say to you ,
 the part I love most of all,
..is every part of you...

IN ONES MIND
2010

In my imagination
I picture you every day
to me you are the perfect woman
perfect in every way

Whenever I think of you
my heart beats faster than before
instead of being in my imagination
I want you to be real - for evermore

HIM AND HER
2007

He liked, what he saw
When they first met
He loved, what they did
When they were together
He, grew tired of her
When the zing had gone
He, stayed out late
Whenever he could
and she
Never stopped loving him

She, liked what she saw
When they first met
She loved, what they did
When they were together
She, never grew tired of him
Even when the zing had gone
She, would not stay out late
Whenever she could
and he
Never understood

IF I COULD
2001

If I had the power to
turn on the light that's hidden within you
and the strength to
lift the dark cloud that blankets your heart
with the might to
release the chains that have bound your emotions
the ability to
unleash the fears that suppress your passion
so that you would
worry not of the future and live for today
perhaps, perhaps then you may understand
how much I love and adore you,
but if I fail
and the past is where you cling
then, one day I will be gone,
Gone, leaving you,
with a heart stifled with remorse
Tear filled eyes
Chasing elusive dreams
An empty bed
No one to love
And still afraid to say
those precious words
"I love you"

AN AIR IN A G STRING
1999

A duet, impromptu,
Lento at first
then cappriccio.
Non tanto,she whispered,
Just leggerio,he sighed.
Without further ado,
Accellanerando...
a murzuka...
Con motto
Allegro
Allegro con motto
Arpeggio
Colla parte
Tremello, !!!!!!
She smiled and hugged him.
"Encore?" He enquired.
"Finis , my virtuoso,"
she said, planissimo.
Then dolce sleep
To dream of their concerto.

NIGHTS
2010

Floating through my haze of dreams
Such a beauty rarely seen
She glows with exquisite charms
I yearn to hold her in my arms
My heart begins to pound and race
As I reach out to touch her perfect face
Alas... In a flash she is gone
I awaken and meet another dawn
Hugging my pillow.

INTIMACY
2010

If all my dreams could come true
to spend the night with you
would satisfy my desire
help ease this inner fire

To let sweet passion rise
we close our eyes
to the world in which we live
and to each other our bodies give
one night of intimacy and caring
a time of love and sharing

Giving free to each other
both surrendering for the another
until our yearnings reach total satisfaction
and join in a simultaneous reaction
of a complete and total climax

KISMET?
2000

Is love, per chance?
pre-ordained, ahead of time?
have fate and destiny
combined to induce their plot
into the hearts of the enamoured?

What mystic threads of love
extend beyond the mortal realm
weaving the tapestry of romance
upon those smitten?

Is it destiny,
unchangeable,
unexplainable and unique...

LOVE AT FIRST SIGHT

The moment he first saw her
Strolling along the pavement
An electrifying tingle ran down his spine
He was awe-struck
There was his perfect dream
Her head held high as she walked
Beautiful legs disappeared into her mini-skirt
Her blonde hair glistening in the sunshine
With heart pounding
His brain spinning
Speechless and numb
What was he to do?
How can he approach this exquisite gazelle
Without startling her away
Then,
With all the courage
He could muster
Unrehearsed
voice quivering
Blurted out
his greatest speech
and said
"Hello"

(on the footpath alongside Ben Nevis – a house that used to be on Adelaide Place)

NOCTURNAL REMINISCE
2012

Another year dissolves into oblivion
memories of their 'once'
stir within heart-held embers
perhaps a little less than before
life now numbed by the humdrum
of an empty daily grind
that now occupies the void
where love once resided

In the small hours of another lonely night
as sleep evades the soul
recollections emanate
among a tangle of yesterdays
yearnings continue unabated
craving to reunite
to replete a pining heart
Questions without answers
preoccupy thoughts until
sleep overpowers the flow
of flickering image replays

REMINDERS
2013

Warm sunny days
remind me of you
watching puppies play
remind me of you
sweet scented flowers
remind me of you
soapy steamy showers
remind me of you
no matter what I do
everything will always
remind me of you

NOCTURNAL SOLILOQUY
1999

A restless night, I lie in bed
Close my eyes,
See images of you
there in the memories, I keep.
I see your eyes,
your sensual smile,
your curling hair.
Hear your voice and
watch your gentle ways.
I imagine you by my side,
I tell you of my love,
How I pine when you're away,
How I want to share your life.
Alas , the images fade.
I reach out to hold you,
But no!!
It's another lonely night...

ONCE AGO
2010

Ever had a secret love?
Hidden in your heart
A love for many years
Of a cherished lover
For reasons torn apart
Should chance arise?
Would one rekindle the flame?
For you and your lost sweetheart
To fall in love again

Would it be a sin?
Maybe deemed old fashioned
To follow ones passion
Relight the flame of a yearning fire
Throw caution to the wind
Set free ones soul
Let your life begin
Discard the shackles of the past
With refreshed heart
Vigor and energy anew
So that now
If only for a while
Enjoy being you

PASSION RISING
2001

We hug,
Two become one
as we hold each other close.
Your sweet essence and soft, soft skin
fill my senses and
sends my heart pounding.
Slowly and tenderly I kiss
your neck, your cheek, your lips.
With your lips echoing my passion.
I become totally lost to you
in this shared embrace,
and wish,
this kiss,
would last forever

THE SWITCH
2001

Turn on the light that's hidden within
Lift the dark cloud that blanket your heart
Release the chains that have bound your emotions
Unleash the fears that suppress your passion
Worry not of the future and live for today
For tomorrow may come and go, in the blink of an eye
Gone, leaving you with a heart filled with remorse
Tear filled eyes
Elusive dreams
An empty bed
No one to love
And once again, afraid to say
"I love you"

SUNSHINE FORECASTED
1999

Should chill winds of confusion
blow into your life
bringing with them
storm clouds of chaos
floods of strife
Blowing from hearts
your love for each other
and the highs you shared
Freezing over
the way you cared
Now, for a time may be parted
with frost upon a chapter of love
that in warm gentle breezes
was started,
Grey clouds of sadness
will dampen your days
chilled by the coldness
of loves gone astray
But raging storms do, in time pass
then from behind thunderclouds
bright sun will shine through
beaming once again, rays of warmth
to the love you once knew.

TEA FOR TWO
2001

He brings to her
a steamy cup of love
sweetened with passion
flavoured with desire
on a tray of hope

She stirs the cup
with fondness and friendship
then lets it go cold
for she does not drink
the tea of love
or the espresso of romance

YOU AND ME
2015

Where to now? he ponders
allowing life's ever changing path
to have its own freedom
to accept whatever may be the outcome.

Hopes and thoughts of a 'maybe-love'
secreted away within,
awaiting events that may unfold,
without fear of gain or loss.

Perhaps this is meant to be
where one is willing
to sacrifice yearning emotions
without ever savoring affection.

That moment of intimate pleasure
from which to seek perspective
or to simply enjoy the experience
in the search for love.

I SEE
2017

When I look into your eyes
I see someone honest and true
When I watch you smile
I see delight and fun
Each time I gaze upon you face
I see a loving soul
When I watch you in the morning
I see a beautiful angel
Everything I see about you
Makes me a very happy
That is why I love you?

LOVE SOMETIMES HAS TO WAIT (song)
2012

Did you ever - find the love?
That you went - looking for
You put our - love on hold
When you walked - out the door

Did you ever - find the life?
You said you - need to find
You left me with - a broken heart
You were always - part of mine

Chorus
When your searching days are over
And your heart is truly free
I wish that you will come back
So I can love you - with you loving me

Did you ever - feel the love?
That you wanted - someone else to give
You will always - be my only love
For as long - as I can live

Has someone - made you happy?
The way you - yearned to be
Is your life - now empty?
Without true love - from me

Chorus
When your searching days are over
And your heart is truly free
I wish that you will come back
So I can love you - with you loving me

TRYING TO WRITE
2014

I wanted to write a poem about you last night...
And every time I tried to put pen to paper
It became my thoughts tangled with emotions caper
Emotions became tangled with my heart
My pen and I couldn't get a start

I was trying so hard to write and then
Random words flowed from the pen
But my mind replayed 'remember when'
The heart, emotions and the words
Got tangled once again

I decided no poetry will I write
Put away the pen tonight
So until we meet again
You will be in my heart to very end
Because you are a wonderful and beautiful friend

SEARCHING FOR THE RIGHT WORD
2014

I wish there was a single word
That would describe someone as beautiful as you
A term that would convey what my heart is thinking
I searched to find that superlative
To no avail
Then as I examined the diamond ring
That I had bought for you
I saw within each glittering facet
The most beautiful colours one could ever imagine
Then at that moment I realised
My search was over
For in my hand
I held that word...
....flawless

HUNTER PROVIDER
2012

Clenched talons grasp
Entrails fur blood
Chisels flesh from bone
Delivers nourishment
Gaping mouths accept
Another meal
Another generation
Perhaps?

ONE FLAG...ONE AUSTRALIA
1995

This flag we raise
To us in many ways
Is the spirit of Australia.

So proud are we
with hearts that are free
in this great country, Australia.

For prosperity we toil
from the sea and soil
our providing land, Australia.

Together we all join hands
with those from many lands
whom now call home, Australia,

and lift our eyes
to the blue southern skies
where our nations flag proudly flies,
above us all, in Australia.

DROUGHT AFFECTED
2000

Water tank empty
The dam has gone dry
No rain for months
Most of the sheep will die.

Feed all gone
Paddock's now bare
Cattle are bony
Dust fills the air.

Farmer's wife waits
Never complains
Hopes and prays
For life giving rains.

IT'S THE BANKS NOW
2013

Sheep and cattle in dire need
Desperate for water and for feed
Hard times have hit the land
Paddocks turned into drifting sand
Months have passed – much of the same
Eyes search the sky
For signs of rain
Hot dry days continue sapping life
From the farmer and his wife
Night after night they would lie in bed
Listen to the thunder - rolling overhead
Waiting for the sweet refrain
The tap, tap, tap of drought breaking rain
Alas for them - it never came

DESPAIR
1999

"I love a sunburnt bloody country of droughts"...
Mud, red mud,
Like thick tomato soup.
Ruts, wheel ruts,
Made by massive big trucks.
Bogged, very bogged,
Right up to the axles.
Miles, many miles.
A long way from anywhere.
...and flooding rains...bugger!!!

THE DROVERS CATHEDRAL
2009

His Church...
The cloudless sky at night...
Glittering with millions of stellar diamonds.

His Choir...
The sound of the bush
As cicada and cricket echo their chorus.

His Altar...
The ancient granite rock on which he places

His Chalice...
A chipped, tea stained enamel mug.

His Communion Wine,
Steaming tea simmering
In the flame-blackened billy
Perched aside the camp-fire.

His Incense...
Smoke that lazily curls upward
From the glowing embers.

His Prayer Mat...
A tattered canvas swag rolled out
On the warm red earth, at dusk
In this heavenly place.

As each new dawn
Appears on the distant horizon, the drover breaks
His bread,
A crusty piece of damper,
And remembers the Body of Christ, and takes
His Communion,
With the Holy Spirit
In vast emptiness of his Australian Outback Cathedral.

DRY AS A LIME-BURNERS BOOT
1999

As I walked towards the shearing shed,
the intense heat of the sun
from a scorching cloudless sky
burned through the back of my shirt.
With each step, red dust rises
floating over my boots.
I brushed the sticky flies from my face
shaded my eyes from the suns intense glare.

The windmill stood motionless,
not a breath of wind passed through its vanes.
The paddocks were now grassless,
Stripped bare of feed
Nothing but acres of parched dirt
For a moment I paused,
to wonder how long it would be
before this soul destroying drought would end
and if I would ever see rain again

SEE'YA LATER MATE
2011

Memories flood the heart
For the man
With a face wrinkled and tanned by time
His soft blue eyes
shaded by that old weather-beaten hat
uniquely him – his trademark
identifiable at a glance
in town, sale-yards, paddocks
a quietly spoken man
never complaining
of hard times, fire, drought
today we said farewell
to natures gentleman
laid to rest
while somewhere out on the farm
the mopokes weep

THE MAGIC OF ELLISTON
2016

From rugged cliff top I watch
Ocean driven breakers
Crash upon the distant reef
That straddles
The entrance of Waterloo Bay
A persistent Westerly breeze
Blows my clothes into disarray
Leaves a salty tang
Coating my lips

A fisherman
In his tinny stands
Rod and reel in his expert hands
Lands another whiting
Children on boogie boards play
The surf looks glorious today
I can only admire the view
Reminisce when me and you
Had fun in former times
When I was
Free from the confines
Of this wheelchair

ALBATROSS
2015

Over the oceans drift
These sailors of the sky
Carried on the winds
Effortlessly lift and glide
On outstretched wings
He wanders his briny domain
Searching for a repast
Of squid, krill and fish

CAMPFIRE
1999

A soft gentle breeze puffs
Wisps of curling smoke
From glowing embers
Friendly flickering flames
A companion fire
A cosy fire

I sit,
Mesmerized, by the pixie-dance of flames.

Without warning
The breeze awakens
Shifts direction
Sparks jump from the coals.
The grass nearby is set alight
Just a few flames at first,
The wind grows stronger
Crimson tongues begin to leap
From grass to bush
From bush to tree
From tree to tree
The bushland is ablaze!!!

Ruby cinders rain
Spawning spot fires
Tinder-dry grasses explode
Merge into a fire-front
Roaring flames
Fanned by an accelerating wind
Burning all in its path
The fire is raging now
Nothing can stop this out of control inferno.

Save me! Save me! I cry
Save the animals
Save the birds
Save the bush from this furnace from hell,
But no one can hear me

I gasp for breath
As kiln-hot air blasts my throat, my lungs
I watch, spellbound,
Powerless against such might,
As the awesome force of hell's flames
Consume all that stand before it...

HEAT
2009

A molten summer sun
oozes up from
the distant hills'
coating the land
in an eerie tangerine glow

Deliberately the fiery orb
detaches itself
from behind its earthly robes
rising into a cloudless blue

The January mercury rising
beyond creature tolerance
Tinder-dry grass and stubble
whisper and stir
as the Northerly wind
announces its malice intent

Throat blistering air
and solar rays hold reign
dominate the land
torture the parched earth

Slowly the blazing radiator
journeys westward across the sky
until the horizon
entombs the astral furnace
into the chasm of night
leaving only the north wind
on it's mission of torment

HE WAS A FISHERMAN
2001

She kissed him on the quayside
waved goodbye once more
his life was on the ocean
hers was on the shore

Many years she did watch and pray
as his boat went off to sea
with two children standing by her side
soon there would be three

Her days were filled with things
a wife could do at home
this time as she waited
she felt there's something wrong

On the phone, sad news came
a boat was lost at sea
"Oh dear God", she cried
"please let no harm befall he".

Boats and planes and folks were called
to search upon the waves
help find the wreck and save the lives,
in vain they searched for days

No trace of boat or crew were found
alas her man was lost
the life that he loved so much
had now come at a cost

Alone she stands on the quay
wishing he would come home
but all that's left is his name
carved in a monument of stone

LAZ'N BACK
2006

takin' life easy
have'n a rest
I'm laz'n back
sufferin' no stress
On the River Murray

goin' with the flow
livin' a life afloat
I'm laz'n back
sailin' a houseboat
Down the River Murray

watchin' the sights
drift'n along
I'm laz'n back
t' the peaceful song
Of the River Murray

wavin' to other folk
livin' the gentle pace
laz'n back too
'way from the rat-race
Cruisin' the River Murray

read'n a good book
enjoy'n a bottle of wine
laz'n back
life's simply fine
Upon the River Murray

MIDDAY SUN
1997

Another outback mid-January day
The mercury sits at 42
My mouth is too dry to raise a spit
I brush the sticky flies from my face
They regroup again and settle on my back

As I walk from the sweltering galvo shearing shed
towards the beckoning shade
of the homestead verandah
The intense heat of the summer sun
burns through my shirt.

I screen my eyes from the suns blinding glare.
sweat soaks the band of my Akubra
trickles down my forehead.
It's too hot to rush
With each slow step, bull dust floats over my boots.

Under the leafy shade of a peppercorn tree,
stretched out on the ochre dirt,
our old black sheepdog lay, panting heavily.
The windmill stands motionless,
not a breath of wind passes through its vanes.

Perched on a fence post, a crow sits
beak held open, gasping to cool itself.
a few bees gathering around the garden tap,
desperately seeking moisture.
Nothing else moves in the scorching heat of this cloudless day,

In the now grassless holding paddock,
the mob of sheep stand huddled
shading their heads under each other
trying to get some relief from the oppressive heat
of the harsh midday sun.

On the verandah,
I turn and look back across the farm
Out of the distant heat-haze shimmer
A dust-devil dances over the paddock
Swirling skywards tinder-dry grass and leaves
Then disappears towards the horizon

I pause, take off my hat
Wipe the sweat from my brow
And wondered if the rain
Would ever come again
And quench this soul destroying drought

PEARSON ISLAND MACROPOD
2009

On this tiny West Coast island
remote from time and reason
tides roll day and night
to sculptured cliffs and granite boulders
massive, rough hewn
by aeons of wind and pounding seas
almost bisecting this pocket of land.

Here, diminutive yellow-faced marsupials
for centuries have endured
in this harsh yet natural place
devoid of fox and feral cat.

These timid sure-footed creatures
have seen explorers, sailors,
sealers and whalers come and go
shared their domain
with sea-lion, petrel and gull
watched fishermen shelter
from windy blusters and tormented swells
under this isolated craggy place.

This scantly wooded outcrop of granite slopes
is crisscrossed by invisible tracks
printed by the soft feet
of the Pearson Island Rock-Wallaby

LIGHTS ON BOSTON HARBOUR
1999

On a summer night in Port Lincoln,
Climb the spiral staircase
To the top of the 'Old Mill',
There, watch the moonlight shine
Across Boston Harbour,
so calm, so beautiful, so still.

See the flashing lights and beacons
Reflecting on the water
Splashing colours of red and green,
Blending with the moon beams
Add enchantment to the scene.

Lights of Fanny Point and Donnington
Safely guiding fishermen
As they sail their way back home
To families friends and lovers
From the ocean that they roam

Streetlights of Tasman Terrace
Their colours shining bright
mirrored on the shoreline,
While ships at the wharf
Load grain into the night.

Yachts anchored on the bay
Silhouetted by the moon,
As coloured globes hoisted high
Up a tall ships mast,
Hang in gay festoon.

Towering floodlit white painted silos
Create a visual backdrop
Where the moon and lights interlace
Gazed upon from this vantage point

              From atop the 'Old Mill'
              In the park on Dorset Place.

SOLS FURY
2009

From Winters Hill they watched
as a summer sun oozed from behind
Boston Island's silhouette
A foreboding tangerine glow
sheened across Boston Bay
until the eastern horizon
detached the fiery orb
to rise slowly but surely
into the transparent sky
The January mercury rose
beyond creature comfort
Anxious eyes monitored
dreading the merest hint of smoke
Tinder dry grass and stubble
whispered and stirred
as the North Wind
announced its malice intention
to those on the hill
that anticipated and waited
hour upon hour
as throat parching heat
held reign
and dominated Eyre Peninsula
while those on the hill
stood guard and squinted
as the sun transited and
tortured the parched earth
Miraculously providence intervened
today's sun finally passed
and sank below
the western horizon
while those on the hill
anticipated a tomorrow
that forecasted the same

STINKY CREEK
2007

If it's a magic weekend you're thinking
Come to Port Lincoln
It's a place of festivity
There's a sign post at the gate way
Saying welcome unto thee

Come there in the spring time
Come there when it's fun time
For the festival of Stinky Creek
It's the reason it's the season
Where lots of people will meet

Join in the music
Join in the dancing
Sing a song or two
If it's lots of laughter is what you are after
Then Stinky is the place for you

Bring your guitar
Bring your banjo
Dress up and have a go
Stand in the spotlight it will be alright
Everyone's part of the show

Share the good food
Share the good times
You'll surely have a ball
On the weekend with lots of great friends

At the Stinky Creek - Folk an Music Festival

Ron Higgins wanted a poem with a reference to Stinky Creek
in it to celebrate the Cellar Folk Club – Stinky Creek Festival

THE LETTER
2006

Received a letter the other day
from a bloke that I once knew
We met some years ago
Just outside of a place named Buckleboo

He drove a header, harvesting fields of grain
While I drove the truck
from the paddock to the silo's,
then back to the paddock again .

The last I heard of him
was from a friend we knew as Jack
Who said me mate had gone up north,
To a cattle station in Queensland's great outback

The letter came from Darwin
where me mate lay in a hospital bed
and he was writin' to let me know
how he broke his bloody leg.

This bloke he was a battler
had to be really bloody crook
for never was a day off work
he'd ever been known to took

First part of the letter he wrote
his bones would take time to mend
now time he had plenty of
to drop a line to a friend

He wrote of the weather
cursing the heat and the rain
For him this was unusual
rarely did he ever complain

In his letter he was saying
'bout how he is now getting old
he said might retire - call it quits
and settle in some place more cold

He'd been doin' a bit of thinkin'
And reckons he might come south
to live near me, his mate
here in Port Lincoln

TIME MARCHES ON
2006

People come, people go,
Different horses, different shows,
Yet, through all things that are changing often,
There's one family held in high regard
and will remain unforgotten,
CLIVE, JULIE, CHRIS, ANTHONY AND TREVOR

People come, people go,
Different horses, different shows,
There will always be some that do their bit
And others that hardly seem to care
But, there's one family that did their share,
CLIVE, JULIE, CHRIS, ANTHONY AND TREVOR

People come, people go,
Different horses, different shows,
From a country farm where peace abounds
To a city supermart with bustle all around,
A family will go,
CLIVE, JULIE, CHRIS, ANTHONY AND TREVOR

People come, people go,
Perhaps with different horses at a different show
We will see you again, somewhere, we hope,
CLIVE, JULIE, CHRIS, ANT AND SPOOK

WOODEN CROSS
1997

A lonely wooden cross stands, next to the highway

as a reminder for us to keep,

placed there to mark the crash site,

where the driver fell asleep.

> When I was driving along National Highway One, I passed a lone wooden cross someone had placed on the roadside, then a fortnight later passed the same spot again. Fresh flowers had been arranged at the foot of the cross. This had a deep effect on me, as the cross was miles from anywhere. The emotions within me, inspired me to write this brief poem.

SOLO VOYAGER
2012

Beyond the horizon
Far from distant shores
With neither sextant nor compass
Intuitively navigating Neptune's realm
Across the seas he roams
Undaunted by wind or storm
Over threatening crest
And plunging trough
This sailor of the sky
The intrepid Albatross
Voyages his briny domain
Freed from the shackles of terra firma

MOTHER NATURE'S MURRAY MORNING
2012

As first pale light peeps through the River Red-gums
Waterfowl open their sleepy eyes
Awaken in their nocturnal lodgings
An occasional squawk, chirp or grunt
Echo through the mist of a Murray dawn
Sudden splash as an unseen Perch, Callop or mighty Cod
Rise to a morning snack of floating morsel.
Among the Bulrushes a mother Black-duck
Quacks a rollcall of her duckling brood.
In the shallows a long-neck turtle paddles furiously
Avoids a sediment-stirring Carp seeking breakfast from the mud.
Motionless, the White-Faced Heron eyeballs
The first meal of the day of unsuspecting frog
Concealed within the reed bed
A Moorhen incubates her clutch of speckled eggs
While a pair of gracious Black Swans survey the state of affairs
As they glide nonchalantly downstream
On a mirror-calm Murray River morning

PERMEATES
2015

In the hot steamy air
Blue-singleted shearers
Arm-wrestle woolly ovine
Into submission
Disrobed of fleece
Chuted to muddy yards
Where shedhands
Daub and delouse
Bewildered quadruped
When days tally complete
The team depart
Taking with them
The subtle whiff
Of lanolin and sweat

SIZE ISN'T EVERYTHING
2013

Under tree I lay
Head pillowed by grasses dry
Eyes focused on leafy limbs above
I listen with intent
To a crystal clear birdcall
Be quick - Be quick - Be quick
Eyes search each branch and shaded clump
For this elusive songster
Be quick - Be quick - Be quick
His cover is momentarily broken
A flit to a nearby twig
To resume his call
Be quick - Be quick - Be quick
This miniscule avian
No larger than a mans thumb
Defies the ratio of size
The Pardalote's hearty call
Resonates among the branches
Be quick - Be quick - Be quick

HEAVENS DAUGHTER
2001

When the gods of the Universe came together
their decision was to create a Goddess
of exquisite sculptured beauty
of grace and elegance
gentle by nature
with a heart of love
the eyes of sincerity
and the spirit of kindness
the soul of an angel
this daughter of the heavens
would be named Selina

FAIRIES AND ANGELS
2013

There are fairies in the garden
Angels in the air
Perhaps you will never see them
But we know that they are there

Fairies make life beautiful
They put the perfume in the flowers
And teach the birds to sing
Just listen in the morning hours

Angels bring together people
By matching kindred hearts
They weave that special magic
That makes the loving start

Whenever you bring your loved-one flowers
Filled with the sweetest of perfume
The angels and fairies
Are with you in the room

BELIEVE IN FAIRIES?
2008

In the very early light of day
During the autumn month of May
As soft sun filters through the leaves
For those of us who do believe
Fairies with gossamer wings
Dance, play and sing...
And if by luck you chance to see
The beautiful Queen Fairy
With golden hair and silver crown
Dressed in a flowing silken gown
Make a wish because Queen Fairies do
Have magic to make your wish come true.

ON GOSSAMER WINGS
2009

Walk quietly into the garden
carefully look around
be very quiet
Try not to make a sound
then you may see
Tiny fairies
With gossamer wings
Playing with their fairy friends
Up among the leaves
Of old almond trees
Amidst the blossoms that bloom in spring

Stand very still
Or sit softly on the ground
Try not to make a sound
then you might hear
tiny fairies
with gossamer wings
Singing with their fairy friends
Melodies of a beautiful fairy song
The one they sing all day long
Amidst the blossoms that bloom in spring

GARDEN CONUNDRUM
2010

How can it be?
My expensive flower and pampered veggie seeds
Do not grow at the speed
Of self-sown unwanted persistent garden weeds

SARAH'S MORNING WALK
2015

"Good morning" barked the dog,
As he ran to fetch the ball
"Good morning" me-owed the cat,
Then she rubbed against the wall

"Good morning" warbled the Magpie
As it flew up in the tree
"Good morning" chirped the Wagtail
Adding a chicka-chicka-chee!

"Good morning" said the butterfly
Landing gently on a flower
"Good morning" said the frog
Splashing in the pond - taking his daily shower

"Good morning all my lovely friends"
Miss Sarah said in return
"Who was it that taught you to speak?
How did you ever learn?"

"It was the Garden Gnome?
From him we learned to talk
He is the one you pass each day
When you go for your garden walk"

"The Garden Gnome?" - replied Miss Sarah
"He has never spoken to me!
Is that because gnomes are very timid
Spends his days just standing under that tree?"

Sarah went to the Gnome and said
"I know that you can speak
Why didn't you say 'Good morning" to me?
From under your big red hat from which you peek"

"Yes I can talk", the Gnome in quiet voice spoke
"I wasn't brave enough because I'm very shy
And it is supposed to be a secret
That's my reason why"

"Don't be frightened or timid" said Sarah
"Your secret is safe with me - I won't tell anyone else
Except the dog, the cat, the frog, butterflies and birds
And maybe the pixies and the elves."

Now, whenever Sarah goes for her garden walk
The Gnome with the big red hat
Would greet her with "Good morning Miss Sarah"
Then spend time together - having a delightful chat.

AMONG THE BLOSSOMS
2013

On a spring time early morning
When the dew is on the ground
Go into your garden
Carefully look around
Be very, very quiet
Try not to make a sound
Look among the flowers
And look up in the trees
If you are quite lucky
You may catch a glimpse of
Our beautiful fairies

Fairies live in gardens
That has lots and lots of flowers
But they only come out
In the early morning hours
To see them you must stand very still
Or sit quietly on the ground
SSSSHH!!!-
Not a movement or a sound
You might even hear them singing
Their beautiful fairy tune
Among the springtime blossoms
Of a garden in full bloom

SUMMER EVENING IMAGES
2011

Moon beams reflect upon the water
beacons flash their red and green
there's a stillness on the harbour
as if floating in a dream

Crystal ripples splash upon the shore
sweethearts walk along the sand
in the stillness of the evening
close together hand in hand

Footprints mark their path
leave a trail as they retreat
two lovers stroll and laugh
make a perfect evening complete

SUMMER EVENING IMAGES 2
2011

Balmy evening airs entwine
With cool sea breezes
Wavelets splash gently on the shore
Softly echo in the silence

Moonbeams on the waters shine
Golden reflections
Across a millpond harbour
Another January days dissolves

Two lovers hand in hand
Leave footprints in the sand
Inner passion rising
Their perfect day complete

Sleepy heads and pillows meet
Tired eyes slowly shut
Gently drift to dreamland
As this summer's day closes

SUMMER EVENING IMAGES 3
2011

Golden moonlight shimmers upon the water
Streetlights encircle the bay
Their reflection shine
Floating on glass

Balmy evening airs converge
With soft sea breezes
Salt scented sea-air lingers
Another January days dissolves

Families promenade the seashore
Children giggle and play
Warm sand under bare feet
As the heat of day
Drifts from memory

SCARY SHADOWS
1993

Sitting in my bed
one dark and stormy night,
when I looked towards the window
it gave me such a fright.
There I saw in front of me,
to my surprise,
was a big boogey monster
ten times my size,
with eyes red and fiery
and teeth big and white,
he looked so black and hairy,
it gave me such a fright.

A monster so large and scary
it made me shiver and shake,
I opened my mouth to scream out,
but no sound could I make.
I grabbed hold of my blankets
quickly pulling them over my head,
but it was still there when I peeped out
so I jumped up and climbed under my bed.

Just then, along came my daddy
into the room and turned on the light,
then I saw it was not a monster
that gave me such a fright.
It was just the moonbeams
shining through a tree,
making scary shadows
that were frightening me.

"Come on now," said daddy,
as he tucked me back in bed,
"It's time to shut your tired eyes
and rest your sleepy head."
Then he closed up the curtains
to keep out the moonlight,
stopping those scary shadows
that gave me that terrible fright.

WE WERE SCARED
2007

Where were you mummy
You left us at home alone
We looked for you
But you had gone
It was late at night
And you weren't in your bed
The car had gone from the shed
Did you go to see that man again?
You told daddy last weekend
That the man was only just a friend
And doesn't mean much to you
You went to see him
Left us all alone
Didn't you!

CHANNELING
2006

Over roof-tops of tile and zinc
Grasping painted fascias
Compilation of aluminium tube and wires
Capture invisible signals
Of information, weather and news
Excitement, horror, fun
Intruded with consume, must have, buy

Reclining bodies with transfixed eyes
Gaze upon cathode and plasma screens
Ingest fact, fantasy, and propaganda
Interrupted with consume, must have, buy
Entertained, brainwashed, ogle, pleasure
Soaps, serials, quizzes, and fake reality
Cooking, gardening, DIY, nature
Interjected with consume, must have, buy

Idle minds feed upon
Boasting, lies and deceit
Fake sincerity, gossip, and voyeurism
Tragedy, humour, sorrow
Interspersed with consume, must have, buy
Ignoring their ability to sever the connection
With simple deft flick of one's finger
On the remote control.

40 YEARS LATER
2006

They Sit

Recliner chairs, slippers on feet, glass of red
Plush pile carpet, split system remote control climate
Plasma digital wide screen TV, remote control
Home theatre - surround sound, remote controlled

Inside

Town house, 4 bedrooms, 3 en suites – with spa, walk in robes
Study, office, formal dining room – 3 car garage, remote control door
Laptop, CD, PC, DVD MP3 with remote control
Boat, caravan, ride on mower, golf buggy, Harley, Superannuated

Together

Dine out 3 nights; take away 3, business lunches 4, quick snacks on Sunday
Cellulite thighs, sagging belly, double d cup, acrylic nails
Beer gut, bald, type 2 diabetes, gout and prostrate problems
Occasional hug, sex rarely, Viagra

And remember

Rented flat, mattress on floor, sheets for curtains, bean bags
Catch the bus, 2 jobs, and steamy sex most days, twice on Sunday
Tupperware parties, Avon, sports bra and aerobic classes
Footy, mates, darts on Wednesday, beer and barbeques
Being young, fit and in love

C'est la vie

40 ANS PLUS TARD
2006

Ils sit

Chaises de Recliner, chaussons sur des pieds, verre de rouge
Tapis de tas cossus, fractionner le système de contrôle à distance climatique
TV numérique sur grand écran plasma, télécommande
Home Cinéma - son surround, à distance contrôlé

À l'intérieur

Maison de ville, 3 chambres, 2 suites fr – avec spa, marcher en robes
Étude, bureau, salle à manger formel – 3 garage automobile, télécommande porte
Portable, CD, DVD MP3 avec télécommande
Bateau, Caravane, ride sur tondeuse, buggy de golf, Harley, Superannuated

Ensemble

Dîner à 3 nuits ; prendre suite 3, déjeuners 4, snacks rapides sur Dimanche
Cuisses de cellulite, ventre, de sagging double d tasse, clous acryliques
Bière intestinale, chauve, tapez 2 le diabète, la goutte et problèmes prostrés
Accolade occasionnel, sexe rarement, Viagra

N'oubliez pas que

Loué matelas sur sol plat, feuilles pour les rideaux, sacs de fèves
Prendre le bus, le 2 emplois, le sexe jaillissants jours la plupart, deux fois le dimanche
Parties Tupperware, Avon, soutien-gorge de sport et aérobic
Footy, camarades, fléchettes, mercredi, bière et barbeques
Étant jeune, ajuster et dans l'amour

Such is life

PASSING DAYS
1999

Listen... Listen, can you hear it
As one thousand years fade away?

Look... Look closely and you will see
The new millennium come into view.

Embrace... Embrace the years that lay ahead
With open hearts and minds.

Welcome... Welcome all that is before you
The challenges and the changes.

Let us all bear witness to passing days,
And all that will be remembered,
The glories, the pains, the joy,
The failures and the triumphs.
This is their final day,
Locked away for ever in a time past.

Now a new millennium arrives.
For you it comes!
A time of opportunity!!
That will last for a thousand years!!!

Behold... It is yours... The Year 2000

WHERE DOES THE WIND COME FROM?
1996

Pray tell?
From whence, doth thy wind bloweth?
From thence, thus come, 'tis quoth...
From whence, thou wind came, 'tis knoweth?
From thence, it blows, thus doth...

MORNING RAMBLER
2011

    I stroll
invading the tranquility
of this secluded bay
    inhale
April's cool air
laced with a salty tang
    glimpse
scrub-wren and honey-eater flit
among the shrubby coastal canopy
    observe
ants scurry with single-minded intent
file upward to sparse autumn blossoms
    watch
godwit and dotrels fox-trot the water's edge
beaks jabbing minuscule morsels
    listen
as crystal wavelets surge
with rhythmic flip-flop
    feel
crusty crisp silica
crunch between my toes
    desecrate
this pristine beach
with today's first human footprints

THE EMBRACE
2000

You can often feel me
As I gently kiss your face,
Alas you cannot hold me
I'm never in one place,
Neither can you see me
When I come close to you
Yet softly I caress your hair
As lovers often do,
One can only hear me
As I go about my way...
Moving the curtains
Gently rustling the leaves
Making flags flutter,
I am, the breeze.

SUNRISE SUZY
2000

As the soft light of a new dawn
slowly filters into the bedroom,
his awakening is greeted
by the gentle tones of her voice.
Warmly cocooned beneath the quilt
he lazes listening
while she tells of her adventures,
sometimes of her childhood
friends and family,
often about the weather
and what's news.
With sleepy eyes slowly opening
he would smile or occasionally laugh
at the funny things said by her,
then, when she was hurt,
feel her pains.
Arise he must from bed
for the day has much to attend.
She too, will go her way,
leaving him, as she does
each morning.
Tomorrow, once again
she will be there
as he awakens
with her soft sweet voice
gently flowing from his bedside radio.

A tribute to Eyre Peninsula local ABC radio presenter, Suzy Grosser.

PERSEVERANCE
2022

Striving to convey to paper,
Those images
Held within the mind
Of memories,
Experiences and fantasy.

Exposing the soul,
To write the emotions of love
Captured within
Its tenderness, excitement and heartache.

The anguish of a frozen pen
Upon a blank paper
Then elation when
A sensual verse is born.
Such is the path of a poet.

I POET
2008

amidst the silence
    patiently I sit
a solitary being
    in this vast universe
armed only with expectation
    quill and parchment
mindfully I plumb the depths
    of my inner self
striving to summons the passion
    within my soul
to compose the lines
    of the most beautiful poem
I have yet to pen

LIMERICKS
2011

There was a young lady that lived at Coffins'
Among the snobs and the boffins
On the share market she was arsey
Now she thought she was so classy
Yet still had holes in her stockings

A Scotsman felt chilled round his knees
But further up parts started to freeze
He was warned about wearing a kilt
And the dangers of having things wilt
In the icy cold Highland breeze

A Scotsman felt chilled round his knees
And that made him start to sneeze
So he said to young lass
With quite a big ass
Can ye sit on my lap lassie please?

WRITERS V CAMERAS CHALLENGE
2006

designer track-suit
pedigree dog
brand-name trainers
morning jog
puffing and sniffing
such humiliation
use the plastic bag
council regulation

bulging eyes
gossamer wings
inside house
annoying things
quick spray
instant kill
decorate now
window sill

3 IMAGES
2008

Peace

Silently the moon
Rose in the sky
Nowhere did it stay
Slowly traveling in an arc
Then vanishing for another day

Harmony

Dulcet notes flow
From her cello
Lingering cords
Sweet and mellow

Commotion

High-pitched guitar screaming
Pounding drums set the beat
Earsplitting amplifier deafening
Leather clad crowd stamping feet
Tattooed Yobbo in microphone shouting
"Youse know who we are??"
Raging horde yells back "Anarchy with a Guitar!!!"

FIRST LETTERS
2010

Last Wednesday
Each month
Tween dinner and bed
Sally's place

Would-be writers gather
Revise homework
Invigorate the mind
Tantalise creativity
Encourage each other

Advance potential

Solutions, ideas
Thoughts
Open to criticism
Rhyme or prose
Yearn to write

EYRE WRITERS
2016

A band of Poets, Authors and Writers would gather
To write to critique and natter
Attend literary learning courses
(With one often sketching horses)
Share expertise for words to combine
Hone the finer points of each chosen discipline
Dione, Mary, Kathy and Christine
Plus Alison, Pat, Aileen and Joy
Helen, Margaret, Dianne and Sally
Just to name a few in this merry tally
With pen in hand and parchment blank
Cogs of their minds begin to crank
Searching for a superlative, perhaps one obscure
Akin to a composer - penning an overture
Their zeal of making rhyme and sentence form
Until a novel, poem or book is born
Away from humdrum house-work each meeting took
Each with a secret desire to create that best seller book.

LIMERICK MUSING
2010

Shop assistant

Selling ladies shoes each day
Is not how she wants to earn her pay
The place she would rather be
On Second floor in haberdashery

Barista

Make Cappuccinos, latte and long black
Take to table and walk back
With empty cups and start again
Every day the bloody same

Fish monger

Squid and Flake and Tommie's too
Nice fresh fish for you
Not so pleasant smell does linger
Here you go smell my finger

Fruiterer

Two bucks a kilo, hear him shout
Get some before they all run out
Never be at this price again
Unless we get some needed rain

I AM THE WIND
1999

Flowing gently through tall ships rigging
Held softly in billowing sails
Caressing those who put their face to me
They, who ride upon the smooth sea,

Yet, if I so choose
Powerful is my mood
Fickle is my nature.

Howling through the yard-arms
Shredding sails as I hurl plumes of spray
Into the faces of those who dared to meet me
Upon my playground, the tormented sea.

If I so choose, I can be a most feared foe
Reckless and untamed.
And yet
If I so choose, I will do your bidding
Serene and gentle

It was I, that brought Tasman, Cook and Flinders
To these shores
It was I, who set the pace
Of the Great Grain Race.

I am here today
Just as I was centuries ago
Yet, I am forever changing,
I AM THE WIND...

BOW YOUR HEADS
1999

Ahoy! All who sail
and fear not of the power of the sea,
listen carefully to the words I say,
or a wet and lonely grave
could be home for you, maybe!

There were those
who lofted sail and hauled on the sheet,
no more they walk the decks
nor sheltered ports they greet.

Men who weren't respectful
to the might of wind and sea,
and deep down in Davey's locker
is where they now lie - silently.

**"Respect the sea,
understand her changing ways.
Be cautious when you sail on her,
don't be fooled by peaceful days...**

**When all is calm
the breeze is light
and the hull gliding through the waves,
for in a moment all could change
and she unleash her fury and her rage..."**

Sails are shredded
and keels upturn
dry cabins are awash.
A lesson of life you will learn,
that the sea is always boss.

Before you weigh the anchor
or cast off from the quay,
Bow your head in deep respect
to the awesome might of the sea.

Bow your heads all you sailors,
Bow your head in quiet respect,
many a man has sailed upon her
and she is not conquered yet!

LIFE IS...
2022

A parade of events
That hone our character
From infancy to maturity
Exploring the gaps between
Of disapproval and acceptance
Honesty and exploitation
Belief and skepticism
Although we
Treasure affection, abhor heartbreak
Relish companionship, endure loneliness
Appreciate vibrant health, encounter sickness
Greet the newborn, say final goodbyes
Accumulate wealth, wrestle poverty
We build, yet destroy
We learn and often forget
Observe others, reflect ourselves
Embrace success, despise failure
Grapple despair, yet always hopeful
That one day we fulfill our dreams.

Such is life.

WHEN I DIE
2024

I will take with me
Every emotion, every learning, every thought
and experience accumulated during my life.
So too, I will carry
each measure of joy, love, sadness and pain
encountered whilst I lived.
My talent, my knowledge, my imperfections, my wisdom
and the essence of my soul
will remain with me - for eternity.

www.ingramcontent.com/pod-product-compliance
Lightning Source LLC
Chambersburg PA
CBHW062041290426
44109CB00026B/2696